MINK SONATA

Allan Havis

I0141360

BROADWAY PLAY PUBLISHING INC
New York
www.broadwayplaypublishing.com
info@broadwayplaypublishing.com

MINK SONATA
© Copyright 1989 by Allan Havis

First published by B P P I in July 1989 in the collection *Plays By Allan Havis*
First printing this edition: December 2011
I S B N: 978-0-88145-511-3

Book design: Marie Donovan
Page make-up: Adobe Indesign
Typeface: Palatino
Printed and bound in the U S A

ABOUT THE AUTHOR

roductions by Allan Havis at San Diego Rep, Old Globe, Vox Nova, Seattle's A C T, Long Wharf, South Coast Rep, American Repertory Theater, Hartford Stage, Virginia Stage, Berkshire Theater Festival, Philadelphia Theater Co, and Rowholt Theater-Verlag (National German Radio). Commissions include England's Chichester Festival, Sundance, San Diego Rep, Ted Danson's Anasazi Productions, South Coast Rep, Mixed Blood, C S C Rep, Malashock Dance, & Carolina Chamber Chorale. With over 15 plays in print, other publications include a novel *Albert the Astronomer*, *American Political Plays* (2001), *American Political Plays After 9/11* (2010), & *Cult Films: Taboo & Transgression*, (2008). In collaboration with composer Anthony Davis, their opera *Lilith* premiered at U C San Diego's Conrad Prebys Hall in 2009. Recipient of Guggenheim, Rockefeller, Kennedy Center/American Express, C B S, H B O, National Endowment for the Arts Awards, & San Diego Theater Critics Circle. He earned an M F A from Yale. He is provost of Thurgood Marshall College/U C San Diego and a professor of Theater.

MINK SONATA was first produced at BACA
Downtown, Brooklyn NY, in September 1986. The cast
and creative contributor were:

CATHERINE..Victoria Boothby
RODNEY..Randy Phillips
ROBERTA & BLAKE..............................Gordana Rashovich

Director...Allan Havis

CHARACTERS & SETTING

ROBERTA—*A girl in her late twenties, slender, delicate with dark hollow eyes. She lives at home with her parents, and has a history of hospitalization. Her voice ranges from great tension to more muted flat tones. There is much innocence to her movements and expressions. She also plays the cello.*

CATHERINE—*ROBERTA's mother. An elegant southern-bred woman in her early fifties. She is fastidious, mannered, coy and clever. Her conceits are plentiful, as are her homilies. She goes into personal campaigns to exert her will. To her credit, she is a sincere Catholic. She fears that she may lose her husband one last time.*

RODNEY—*ROBERTA's father. A short, balding man around sixty. He is affable, off beat, a drinker, a practiced speaker. By profession, a political media consultant. His disposition fluctuates between genuine concern for others to rich executive aloofness. His lust is clumsy and paternal.*

BLAKE—*ROBERTA's alter ego. She is stylish, self-confident, and very attractive. In image and attitude, the direct opposite to ROBERTA.*

A large rambling west side apartment in New York City

PRODUCTION NOTE

ROBERTA and BLAKE are played by the same actress.

The play begins with a Prologue with the three actors in white masks taking part in three imaginary photo sessions. They pose together with RODNEY in the middle. The Prologue should last no longer than one minute. Music for prologue might be foreign percussion or environmental music of abstract nature.

To allow for the elaborate costume changes between BLAKE/ROBERTA, rear screen projection and images of a woman against a screen of stretch fabric (seeing relief of her hands, breasts and face etc. in motion) are suggested: silhouettes of a woman playing a cello in frenzy, of a woman holding up the see-through masks and turning to one over the other (as if rejecting one mask), and of a man and woman coming together for an embrace.

For the scene in ACT ONE where BLAKE and ROBERTA talk to each other, it is suggested that the actress address children's dolls to represent surrogates of BLAKE and ROBERTA. The actress might wear a mask for half of the scene (as well as stay with the dolls for half of the scene) until she moves to speak into an imaginary mirror facing the audience. On the line, "You mustn't be harsh," the actress might talk over a pre-recorded tape with her voice saying the same line... as if an echo were heard.

Solo cello music from Bach is suggested to link the scenes together between and during blackouts. Sinatra music may be heard at the start-up of ACT TWO, Scene One. The song itself should be romantic and melancholic.

to Cecil Lytle—
for the passion of good music and art

ACT ONE

Scene One

(From her bedroom, CATHERINE—still dressing herself—joins RODNEY in the living room. RODNEY is reading on the couch.)

CATHERINE: *(Rushed)* Yes, in an hour. We're supposed to have dinner with the Farrows. It's theme night at Harriet's.

RODNEY: Harriet again? What shall I wear?

CATHERINE: Anything but your red blazer. You wore that last time.

RODNEY: Is Roberta coming?

CATHERINE: No.

RODNEY: *(Innocently)* Why not?

CATHERINE: Her little pets are crapping everywhere.

RODNEY: Oh?

CATHERINE: They've soiled every rug in here, Rodney.

RODNEY: Doesn't the girl vacuum?

CATHERINE: My priceless Belgium rugs, Rodney. *(Turning from a full length mirror)* I won't have it in my house!

RODNEY: Calm down, Catherine. I'll discuss it with her.

CATHERINE: *(Still fuming)* Damnit! They'll kick us out of the co-op if this continues! Word has gotten out.

RODNEY: That's not a problem.

CATHERINE: She's the oldest boarding school girl in the world. No real maturity. No friends. No dates. A complete failure.

RODNEY: *(Kindly)* Were you fighting today? *(Silence. Gets up)* I'd like a brandy.

CATHERINE: I'd like her pregnant. I don't like lesbians for prep girls.

RODNEY: Many girls may seem that way.

CATHERINE: She can't hide it from me. The odd vacant way she stares. Her bizarre make-up. She keeps changing her style of clothes. Haven't you noticed?

RODNEY: It's her age, darling. Wait until her thirtieth birthday.

CATHERINE: Lesbians are never happy.

RODNEY: What did you do with the brandy?

CATHERINE: They don't have real lives. They connive. They keep cats and birds and hide away in rent control apartments in Chelsea. And they have churches and doctors for themselves with spurious mailing lists. They do, Rodney, they do. I ran into Updike, the writer, at my doctor's. We talked. He says it's all true. And Rodney, he said it was your fault. *(Sudden switch)* My thyroid's acting up. Come see.

RODNEY: *(Approaching, with a gentle touch)* Is it? *(Pause)* So you met Updike?

CATHERINE: I did.

RODNEY: Is his daughter a lesbian?

CATHERINE: He didn't say. *(Pause)* I don't think I'm hysterical. It's just that I...I love Roberta very much.

You'd think she'd realize this. I shower her with love and affection. Isn't that so, Rodney?

RODNEY: Yes, Catherine.

CATHERINE: And not a recent love. A love which flowered over the years. *(Affectionate caresses to* RODNEY*)* We should fly away, take a long vacation.

RODNEY: You know I don't want one.

CATHERINE: Just the two of us.

RODNEY: My work won't allow us.

CATHERINE: Our marriage calls for it.

RODNEY: It is my fault. I've probably been remiss.

CATHERINE: Then let's find her a fabulous place to live.

RODNEY: You know how fragile she is, Catherine.

CATHERINE: Why don't we buy her a Samari sword or a Saturday night special?

RODNEY: Don't be absurd tonight.

CATHERINE: Was I being absurd? *(Kisses* RODNEY *playfully)* Then let us move. Leave her this apartment. She can have the darling rugs.

RODNEY: But I entertain here.

CATHERINE: There are suites everywhere in town. Or we could even leave the city. I don't care for New York any longer. I dislike all our neighbors. The elevators decapitate. The electrical wiring is in Swahili. The night doorman has scurvy.

*(*ROBERTA, *having entered from her bedroom, interrupts.)*

ROBERTA: He's a decent respectable doorman.

CATHERINE: Then why does he wrap his trouser belt around like a Mexican bandit? And why does he always drink from a paper bag?

ROBERTA: He's eccentric, Catherine. Everyone's eccentric in this building.

CATHERINE: Yes, I can believe that. Roberta, do you want this apartment all to yourself?

ROBERTA: Why do you ask?

CATHERINE: Your father and I were thinking about moving across the river.

RODNEY: But I entertain here.

CATHERINE: Stay out of this Rodney.

ROBERTA: But we're New Yorkers, Catherine.

CATHERINE: There are New Yorkers in Nicaragua. We could live in Saddle River. Wouldn't a garden be nice? Raise tomatoes, turnips...

RODNEY: *(Mock conspiratorial to* ROBERTA*)* Humor her. *(Crosses to his bedroom)* If you'll excuse me, I'll get ready for Harriet's.

ROBERTA: Can I go with you?

CATHERINE: No, dear.

ROBERTA: Why not?

CATHERINE: Couples only. So sorry.

ROBERTA: I don't want to be alone this evening.

CATHERINE: Play your cello.

ROBERTA: Catherine, don't be cutting.

CATHERINE: I keep insisting you try to make some friends. Friends keep us happy. Let's make an effort to be social! Take up ballroom dancing, Roberta.

*(*CATHERINE *and* ROBERTA *exchange looks carefully.)*

CATHERINE: Expect us home early...but don't wait up for us. *(Abruptly)* Did you buy the anti-pasta?

ROBERTA: No.

CATHERINE: What about all the chick peas in the fridge?

ROBERTA: For the minks.

CATHERINE: Is that what makes them crap so much?

ROBERTA: No, it's your interior decorating.

CATHERINE: Don't be cute darling. It makes you fetching. I urge you to get these shitty beasts out of the house in forty-eight hours. Or else...

ROBERTA: Or else what?

CATHERINE: A plague will descend upon us from the bible. *(Pause)* When are you getting a husband?

ROBERTA: Never.

CATHERINE: Marriage would elevate you to great heights.

ROBERTA: I don't like heights.

CATHERINE: Nor do I. At least we agree about some things.

ROBERTA: We agree about Rodney.

CATHERINE: Do we? *(Pause)* I'm going to throw you on the auction block someday, young lady.

ROBERTA: Why must I marry?

CATHERINE: Life calls for marriage. Your grandmother didn't want a husband but wasn't unhappy. She ran the marriage like a little boutique. *(Pause)* No, I never met a happy spinster. One day you'll wear my wedding dress. It's so wonderfully sheer. We'll take in the bust and improve the hips. Fill out your valleys. And the veil...

ROBERTA: Weddings are so depressing.

CATHERINE: Mine wasn't. Your father was the loveliest bridegroom.

ROBERTA: I can imagine.

CATHERINE: Aren't you seeing someone? That dire Jewish violinist from Philadelphia?

ROBERTA: I'm in love with the dumbwaiter.

CATHERINE: One day you'll wear my gown, darling. You will become a bride in full regalia.

ROBERTA: You scare me, Catherine.

CATHERINE: As you scare me, darling. Which proves we're related. If you stop scaring me, I'll stop scaring you. *(New smile)* Companionship, I cannot stress that enough.

ROBERTA: I have my cello.

CATHERINE: Which do you really prefer, little Cinderella? Linseed oil for your cello, or men's cologne?

ROBERTA: Animal manure.

CATHERINE: Why must you be contrary?

ROBERTA: I can't stop myself.

CATHERINE: It's a miracle that you can keep up with the orchestra.

ROBERTA: Yes, it's a miracle.

CATHERINE: I must get ready for tonight. *(Trying to excuse herself)* Do clean up your bedroom. And the newspapers in the cages.

ROBERTA: Yes, Catherine. *(Eye contact holding)* You spoil every Christmas.

CATHERINE: I'm very fond of Christmas. Don't we always pick out the grandest tree for the living room? Don't we go carolling? What would you like for Christmas, darling?

ROBERTA: A gargoyle from Prague.

CATHERINE: *(Deadpan)* But Roberta, we got that for you last year.

ROBERTA: Leave me alone.

CATHERINE: Is this our thanks for sending you to an epicurean boarding school?

ROBERTA: I don't know, Catherine.

CATHERINE: You happen to be a beautiful girl. Why must you punish us like this?

ROBERTA: I hate sex.

CATHERINE: Yes, I know.

ROBERTA: You don't know.

CATHERINE: It's so simple really. You bring flowers. He brings wine.

ROBERTA: When I think of it, I hear the gnawing of little bony teeth.

CATHERINE: Well darling. You'll have to think of something more pleasant.

ROBERTA: The pounding of decaying flesh is rather unsightly, don't you think?

CATHERINE: There's candle light, or those novelty blindfolds your father's so very fond of.

ROBERTA: Your mattress creaks like a decrepid sausage machine.

CATHERINE: Do you really stay up all night, Roberta?

ROBERTA: I do. I require no sleep.

CATHERINE: You should sleep. You need your sleep.

ROBERTA: Sleep is brutal. Like sex. I'd rather sing a ballad.

CATHERINE: That simply won't do. *(Pause)* I don't like your innuendos, dear. I think you should start getting

dressed and remove the charming bird's nest from
your hair. We may have company tonight.

ROBERTA: I'm ill. Let me count the ways. Agoraphobia.
Stigmata. Anorexia.

CATHERINE: *(Oblivious to* ROBERTA*)* I'm ordering
drapes. The rodents go. Immediately. I want the rugs
washed and your room fumigated.

ROBERTA: They're minks. They're my friends.

CATHERINE: I'll buy you a fur. Anything in my closet
is yours. You realize this represents a mild behavior
disorder. If you're depressed we'll get you lithium.

ROBERTA: The ancient cure for step-mothers was
bloodletting.

CATHERINE: I'm your mother. Not your step-mother.
I know you want to be rid of us. As soon as you toss
your head, I know. And when you get destructive I
seem to be right behind you. *(Silence)* Would you ever
let me kiss you? *(Pause. She changes strategy.)* We're
supposed to have visited the Farrows, but set the table
for four. We've company.

ROBERTA: Who's coming?

CATHERINE: A student of your father's. I really know
little about it. Please make yourself presentable.

*(*CATHERINE *busies herself at* RODNEY*'s study.* ROBERTA
exits to her bedroom. In a moment CATHERINE *exits. Then*
RODNEY *enters toward the bar.* BLAKE *enters from the other*
corridor. She wears clothes distinct from ROBERTA*.)*

RODNEY: Can I offer you a drink?

BLAKE: Thank you.

RODNEY: How was your flight?

BLAKE: On time.

RODNEY: Didn't you have red hair at Amherst?

BLAKE: Yes. I thought another tint would do well.

RODNEY: I think so. You look absolutely delectable. Have you plans for the holidays?

BLAKE: None.

RODNEY: *(With briefs under his arms)* I read these things rather frequently.

BLAKE: If it's inconvenient I'll come back another day.

RODNEY: You really should have phoned my office. My wife makes a point of these things.

BLAKE: I can understand.

RODNEY: Though she likes when I work at home, we've a policy about visitors. *(Hands her drink. Silence)* Exactly how did we meet?

BLAKE: You were visiting the college as a lecturer.

RODNEY: And I invited you here?

BLAKE: Yes.

RODNEY: That is unorthodox of me. You say you're a journalist?

BLAKE: Actually a political science major.

RODNEY: Where have you worked?

BLAKE: The Farmer's Almanac.

RODNEY: I'm not hiring at this time.

BLAKE: Perhaps if you saw my work.

RODNEY: Really...

BLAKE: *(Persistent)* I want to work for you, Mr. Alexander. I believe in you. I'm very good with cameras and lights.

RODNEY: Are you?

BLAKE: Let me intern under you.

RODNEY: You're most lovely, and I would be flattered to have you on my staff, but it's really not possible.

BLAKE: If it's my age...

RODNEY: I don't hire women, it's that simple. If I led you to believe otherwise, please accept my apologies. Stay for dinner. You did go out of your way to come here. We'll set another place at the table. *(He abruptly dismisses her, and begins to read.)* If you care to, why not stay for the holidays? We've plenty of room.

(CATHERINE enters with coffee tray and cups.)

BLAKE: *(Acknowledging CATHERINE)* I like your home.

CATHERINE: Thank you.

BLAKE: And what a stylish Christmas tree.

CATHERINE: From the Governor.

BLAKE: I do hope it snows. Christmas is such a joyful occasion.

CATHERINE: We love Christmas. It's the only time when my husband isn't at work. He never vacations. He schedules his heart attacks between election years.

BLAKE: Is it his Havana cigars?

CATHERINE: *(Solicitous)* Rodney, I've an ally.

(RODNEY is ignoring them for the moment.)

CATHERINE: How did you like Amherst?

BLAKE: Very much.

CATHERINE: Our daughter went to Amherst. She's a musician. Do you know her? A prodigy at age four. She's won countless awards. So incredibly gifted. *(Shows photo of ROBERTA on mantle)* As a child she walked up to a cello and began playing like a master. How frightened we were. What powers she possessed. Like Casals she could butcher the instrument or torture an audience. The darling girl plays for keeps.

Scene Two

(Later that evening)

RODNEY: *(At his desk, doing his slow burn.)* Don't touch my things, Roberta. My desk is impossible as it is. You know I can't tolerate confusion.

ROBERTA: *(Difficulty with her unfastened dress. Slants over RODNEY)* My zipper's stuck, please...

RODNEY: *(Responding delicately)* There. Now leave me in peace. *(She lingers like a forlorn cat.)* What is it you want?

ROBERTA: Nothing.

RODNEY: Why don't you help your mother entertain?

ROBERTA: She doesn't need me. *(Silence)* I realize I'm not your favorite.

RODNEY: I never said that.

ROBERTA: I'm not from another planet, Daddy. Did you really think I was?

RODNEY: Never.

ROBERTA: Still...

RODNEY: Darling, we've company tonight.

ROBERTA: Get rid of her.

RODNEY: Don't be petulant.

ROBERTA: Why do you like this girl more than me?

RODNEY: Who said anything of the sort?

ROBERTA: Then why is she here?

RODNEY: I'm a lecturer at Amherst.

ROBERTA: What has that to do with it?

RODNEY: *(Still annoyed at the interruption)* We're just extending our hospitality to a visitor. After all, she is from your alma mater.

ROBERTA: Do you think I'm from the sea like Ondine? Or was a difficult birth under an alien comet? Am I an alien? You used to read to me from Hans Christian Anderson in so many voices. Remember? The old farting gnome dancing around with his young bride? And little Thumbelina?

RODNEY: Yes, I remember.

ROBERTA: Christmas is like a fairy tale. Have you seen I've decorated the tree?

(RODNEY's attention returns to the desk.)

ROBERTA: I don't want to go to church this Christmas.

RODNEY: *(Not looking up)* Why not?

ROBERTA: Because I'm lewd.

RODNEY: No, darling.

ROBERTA: Oh, but I am. I cook soup lewder than anyone. That's what Catherine thinks. I can read her thoughts. *(Sits on his desk like a teenager)* I think you're lewd.

RODNEY: *(Looking up)* Why?

ROBERTA: Look at your soup. *(Pause)* You remind me of Evelyn Waugh with a Brooklyn accent.

RODNEY: I've lost my Brooklyn accent. And stay off my desk, Roberta.

ROBERTA: I'll never marry you, Daddy.

RODNEY: Why are you acting so strange tonight?

ROBERTA: Maybe your daughter is confused.

RODNEY: Why are you confused?

ROBERTA: *(Sweetly)* I've been out of the hospital less than a year.

RODNEY: It's time I stop doing somersaults when you cry for me.

ROBERTA: I used to cut my hair every day like a superstition. Superstitious about the water in my bath. About the water in my drinking glass. I'm superstitious about swallowing sperm. I was deathly scared of tongue kissing. I thought men had pastel chalk on their little skin. I did.

RODNEY: You do this to amuse me. I am not amused. Your mother thinks we embellish.

ROBERTA: We do.

RODNEY: That we are overly involved with each other. You know she goes to Saint Thomas every day. If only you could understand. (Pause) Alone at night, it becomes an unveiling. (Pause) Go put some make-up on. It'll do you good.

ROBERTA: For you?

RODNEY: For me.

(ROBERTA kisses RODNEY lightly on the chin, kicks off her shoes, prances out to her room.)

RODNEY: She's so troubled.

(CATHERINE enters in a stunning dress.)

RODNEY: You look radiant, Catherine.

CATHERINE: Thank you, Rodney.

RODNEY: Where do you find these garments?

CATHERINE: Slumming through Bergdorf Goodman's. (Pause) Dinner will be ready shortly. One of those fifteen second casseroles. How long is this girl staying with us?

RODNEY: It's up to you.

CATHERINE: Do you mean that?

RODNEY: Yes.

CATHERINE: Very well then. The guest room is ready. *(Pause)* Tell me what you want for Christmas, Rodney.

RODNEY: May I split my wish?

CATHERINE: No, that's cheating. *(Stroking* RODNEY's *hair from behind)* You must pay more attention to me at home. No more late night excuses. You were such a flirt as a young man. Ever since your equestrian injury your posture has changed. You sit like a member of royalty. So erect. *(Pause)* I'm thinking of going into business, darling. You needn't worry. I plan to use my maiden name.

RODNEY: Why do you want to compete with me?

CATHERINE: If I wanted to compete with you I'd have an affair with a close relation.

RODNEY: You've had many affairs.

CATHERINE: Hardly.

RODNEY: Catherine...

CATHERINE: Can you count them?

RODNEY: Must I?

CATHERINE: I'm in analysis. We count in analysis.

RODNEY: Don't give me your sad dog looks, darling. No journals. This is silly. Your editorial skills— excellent they may be—are from another age. Nor are they warranted.

CATHERINE: I want to be a public person, just like you.

RODNEY: I don't like our being public.

CATHERINE: I thought about writing children's books, but who knows what they're reading? I prefer your kind of work.

RODNEY: You want to emulate your father.

CATHERINE: Maybe so. He gave you your chance in politics, Rodney.

RODNEY: And I am forever grateful to him.

CATHERINE: Father treasured your enthusiasm. Why not lend some to me?

RODNEY: Politics is not glamorous. It's a back room affair. Always dirty.

CATHERINE: And therefore you'll tutor this lost debutante?

RODNEY: I asked for your opinion.

CATHERINE: What choice did I have?

RODNEY: You had a choice. You still do. Everyone has a choice. *(Pause)* And you made a good choice. *(Pause)* Why not send her in?

CATHERINE: Crash course tonight?

RODNEY: Yes.

CATHERINE: What's your hurry?

RODNEY: New agenda, no hurry.

(RODNEY turns his back to CATHERINE as she exits. In a few moments BLAKE enters, in loose seductive clothes.)

BLAKE: *(At RODNEY's desk, clearing a space)* My first day on the job.

RODNEY: *(Not directly looking)* Come in with a dress.

BLAKE: A pants suit?

RODNEY: We start with a dress.

BLAKE: But Mister Alexander... *(Long pause. She puts on a casual house coat.)* I'm ready.

RODNEY: Sit at the couch. We shall take polls today.

BLAKE: Polls?

RODNEY: You mustn't ask questions. *(Pause)* Begin with an interview.

BLAKE: Interview who?

RODNEY: The mayor.

BLAKE: The mayor? What do I ask the mayor?

RODNEY: Anything.

BLAKE: The mayor of New York? *(Pause)* Can I ask him about his personal life?

RODNEY: Yes. Stop toying with your necklace.

BLAKE: Mister Mayor, can you explain why most of your friends are under indictment?

RODNEY: What does he say?

BLAKE: I don't really know.

RODNEY: He'd make you laugh.

BLAKE: Then I'd make a joke too.

RODNEY: No, don't. The mayor can't take jokes.

BLAKE: I can at least try to please the mayor.

RODNEY: He expects you to. Can you charm him?

BLAKE: I'll ask him into the studio for a drink.

RODNEY: Good. These last few weeks he's looked a mess.

BLAKE: Leave him to me.

RODNEY: What about the mayor do you want to capture on camera?

BLAKE: His cheap irony. He upsets me.

RODNEY: Why does he upset you?

BLAKE: Because he looks like a gay mobster.

RODNEY: Why does he look like a gay mobster?

BLAKE: It could be his tailor.

RODNEY: Anything else?

BLAKE: He has a habit of wincing.

RODNEY: And what can you do?

BLAKE: I'd lick the wincing.

RODNEY: How?

BLAKE: I'd drug the son-of-a-bitch.

RODNEY: *(Kindly)* I think you're a natural. *(Pours two glasses of brandy. He stops her from touching her drink, and then reproaches her mildly.)* There's a girl who follows me home after work. She's rather shy. I spoke to her before getting into my cab. She smiled rather passively. We stared at each other. I said if you're going to follow me...it will cost you dearly. It happened as if it were a dream. But I expect her now, casually, like the proverbial leopard in the corner.

(RODNEY nods, allows her to pick up her brandy. They drink together, cautiously. BLAKE sets her glass down, leave the couch slowly.)

RODNEY: You may think the worse of me.

(BLAKE exits, then ROBERTA enters.)

ROBERTA: I don't want anyone touching you, Daddy.

RODNEY: Don't worry, darling.

ROBERTA: I can't help it.

RODNEY: You like to worry.

ROBERTA: Am I spoiling something?

RODNEY: Your mother wants me to pretend. How can I pretend? *(Drinking absently)* Maybe it was our days in the kitchen.

ROBERTA: You want me to move out?

RODNEY: Yes.

ROBERTA: It's because of Catherine. Why doesn't she move out?

RODNEY: It's time you lived with friends.

ROBERTA: I have no friends.

RODNEY: You're too old for finishing school.

ROBERTA: No more therapy.

RODNEY: No one said therapy.

ROBERTA: But I know what you're thinking, Daddy.

RODNEY: Do you?

ROBERTA: A stately mansion with rolling hills and closed circuit TV. Have you really tired of me? Daddy?

RODNEY: Darling, I'm at wit's end.

ROBERTA: Come to my window at night.

RODNEY: And then what?

ROBERTA: We'll elope. That's what you really want.

Scene Three

(Later that evening. At CATHERINE's *door)*

BLAKE: *(Embarrassed)* I'm sorry, Mrs Alexander.

CATHERINE: I thought I left it locked. You must be lost.

BLAKE: You must think I'm awful.

CATHERINE: Your room is two doors down. I do hope you're comfortable here. *(Pause. Seeing something in* BLAKE's *hand)* May I ask you something, dear? What do you want with us?

BLAKE: Must I answer?

CATHERINE: Do you feel superior?

BLAKE: Hardly.

CATHERINE: No offense, darling. But young women are simply nauseating. *(Studying her sharply)* Will you sell copy to the newspapers?

BLAKE: No.

CATHERINE: You could make a lot of money. You know what I'm talking about. You ruin good families. This is a good family.

BLAKE: I realize.

CATHERINE: In due time you'll be given an office and staff. He'll give you more power than you need, or deserve.

BLAKE: *(Resisting)* I've something to say to you.

CATHERINE: You needn't.

BLAKE: Madam, I must.

CATHERINE: My husband is not your concern.

BLAKE: I had an affair with him at school.

CATHERINE: How delightful. Credit or non-credit?

BLAKE: I'm quite serious.

CATHERINE: Rodney likes a little recreation. It does wonders for him. Makes him feel frisky, like a puppy in the country. But understand, he cannot fall in love. We've been to all the therapists and circus wisemen.

BLAKE: He's in love.

CATHERINE: No, no. It's your vanity, that's all. *(Pause)* My dear, you don't realize we're married over thirty years. Our life together chugs on. You're the hitchhiker.

BLAKE: I love your husband deeply.

CATHERINE: I'm flattered.

BLAKE: *(Pause)* He told me you were dying.

CATHERINE: Did he really? *(Pause)* Do you believe that?

BLAKE: I don't know what to believe.

CATHERINE: I'm dying of boredom. Do I get any sympathy?

BLAKE: I'm not here to undo your home. I love your home.

CATHERINE: If you care for my husband, obey me to the letter.

BLAKE: How do you mean?

CATHERINE: You're such a sweet thing, really. *(Touches* BLAKE *quickly)* Sweetness can bring down an empire. You mustn't. Promise me you won't.

BLAKE: I promise.

CATHERINE: Now no more talk about Rodney. Trust me to look after your interests. I will not disappoint you.

*(*CATHERINE *her to her room. Crosses to couch where* RODNEY *is napping. She wakes him.)*

CATHERINE: Were you sleeping, darling?

RODNEY: Yes. In the middle of a dream.

CATHERINE: Roberta is failing. She's no better than her time away at the clinic.

RODNEY: I see, Catherine.

CATHERINE: We've become hostages to each other. She must leave.

RODNEY: You wish this every Christmas.

CATHERINE: I get depressed with every holiday. She makes me so sullen.

RODNEY: If Roberta moves her playing will end. Nine dead fingers. You must respect her cello. There's a rare and wonderful gift in her. What will happen to her hands, Catherine?

CATHERINE: Let them petrify.

RODNEY: Bite your tongue.

CATHERINE: I might bite you in a moment.

RODNEY: Admit you're jealous.

CATHERINE: I wish my father were alive.

RODNEY: Insouciance, he would say, like a parrot.

CATHERINE: You make a joke of his memory.

RODNEY: *(Caressing* CATHERINE's *hair)* I'm sorry, Catherine. But you're so very mean to the child.

CATHERINE: I'm not dead.

RODNEY: Who said you were?

CATHERINE: You.

RODNEY: To my contemporaries, you appear to be.

CATHERINE: How comical you are, Rodney.

RODNEY: Am I?

CATHERINE: And yet I'm devout to you. A subordinate. It's time to change all that.

*(*CATHERINE *away from* RODNEY.*)*

RODNEY: Very well, Catherine.

(Lights dim over them, and rise near ROBERTA's *bedroom. She appears with some of* BLAKE's *clothes mixed in hers. The following dialogue is delivered with equal distance from both characters.)*

BLAKE: I so very admire your father. He can slay most any sacred cow without vulgarity. Only Jesus was more deft.

ROBERTA: Many people admire him.

BLAKE: Tell me the truth, Roberta. *(Pause)* Did you ever...

ROBERTA: No.

BLAKE: I'm afraid it's an involuntary pregnancy. Many astronauts gain in flight.

ROBERTA: I'm glad I'm dieting for I was once pregnant.

BLAKE: What's that sound?

ROBERTA: Minks.

BLAKE: *(Pause)* I could change your make-up. Stop your chin from receding. We can tweeze, add some eye shadow. Your lips are so thin and pale, like a child under cold water. Lift the hair off the neck. Such a lovely neck. We could, Roberta. I could be your little sister. We could shower together, pretend to be oriental, Find the horse bridle. Move the hands. Drop blood on clean linen.

ROBERTA: You mustn't be harsh.

BLAKE: Of course.

ROBERTA: At school I was not jubilant. I was going to die for my period. The few boys I took home were all insane.

BLAKE: I once took home a walrus.

ROBERTA: Three feet on the floor if you please.

BLAKE: The boys I took home were not permitted to have oral sex. So I developed a taste for oysters. *(Pause)* Then a married man came my way.

Scene Four

(Moments later. ROBERTA *comes into the living room with her bags.)*

ROBERTA: I'm all packed.

CATHERINE: So quickly, darling? I was going to help you.

ROBERTA: No, you don't.

CATHERINE: I hope you didn't take my good towels.

ROBERTA: Rest assured, I didn't.

CATHERINE: I'm so excited, Roberta. Such a big moment in our life. It feels like we're sending you off to summer camp.

ROBERTA: *(Acidic)* Do I get visiting privileges, Catherine?

CATHERINE: What sort of question is that?

ROBERTA: You've made a million rules for me.

CATHERINE: Of course you've visiting privileges. You're only a few blocks away. I'll take the cross town bus to see you. We'll use the same dry cleaners. What rules have I made up? *(Helping her pack the last box in the living room.)* Am I overbearing? *(Pause)* Yes. I must be. You don't deserve this treatment. Forgive me. Your father is so frail. The two of you have eclipsed my world.

ROBERTA: Am I the only one leaving?

CATHERINE: Yes, darling.

ROBERTA: She's moving in?

CATHERINE: Only temporarily.

(RODNEY enters in a smoking jacket.)

ROBERTA: *(Plaintively)* Daddy!

RODNEY: What, sugar?

ROBERTA: That bitch is taking my place?

RODNEY: No one is taking your place.

ROBERTA: If I was a distraction, what will she be?

RODNEY: *(Approaching ROBERTA)* You were never a distraction. Why be so hard on yourself?

ROBERTA: *(About to cry)* You're making me crazy.

RODNEY: Please, Roberta. Be a big girl now. Catherine, would you please say something?

CATHERINE: It's your father's very own cadenza.

RODNEY: Catherine...

CATHERINE: Your father wants a plaything for the office. That's all it is. That's all it will be.

ROBERTA: I'll never love you again.

RODNEY: You don't mean that.

ROBERTA: *(Crying)* I do.

RODNEY: These are growing pains. We all go through them. How well I know mine. But the upsets fade. Something in nature heals us. Roberta, let nature take her course.

ROBERTA: I want to die.

RODNEY: *(His arm around her, consoling.)* Cheer up. I hate to see you this way.

CATHERINE: Are the minks in their cage?

ROBERTA: No.

CATHERINE: Please lock them up now.

ROBERTA: I don't have to. They're all dead.

CATHERINE: Oh, did you poison them?

ROBERTA: Yes. You gave me the poison.

CATHERINE: Just as well. *(Pause)* I hope you packed your wedding dress, my poor darling.

END OF ACT ONE

ACT TWO

Scene One

(Some weeks later)

RODNEY: *(At the bar)* Would you like some wine?

BLAKE: Bourbon.

RODNEY: On the rocks?

BLAKE: Please.

RODNEY: *(Bringing the drinks to the couch)* I'd like to set up an observatory on the terrace. Install a high powered telescope. Study my neighbors from a correct distance.

BLAKE: That would be amusing.

RODNEY: Not that I'm a voyeur. I disapprove of voyeurism. Do you have a hobby?

BLAKE: I keep a journal.

RODNEY: What do you write in your journal?

BLAKE: Odd things.

RODNEY: Specifically?

BLAKE: Miscreant epitaphs.

RODNEY: You don't seem the criminal sort.

BLAKE: I'm not. Are you?

RODNEY: That's a difficult question.

BLAKE: Are you criminal?

RODNEY: If you mean for personal gain...no, I'm not criminal. My profession is another matter.

BLAKE: You pass as a white collar criminal, don't you?

RODNEY: No. I don't wish to be. *(His arm around her)* Campaigns can be ethical.

BLAKE: I've never witnessed one.

RODNEY: You've become a cynic. Have I made you one? There are no true forms with our electorate. Hawks are doves. Liberals are John Birchers. A Neanderthal can turn progressive. For every position there are two candidates from the same cloth.

BLAKE: Which cloth am I?

RODNEY: A modern cloth.

BLAKE: What does that mean?

RODNEY: That you're durable.

BLAKE: I don't want to be alone, Rodney.

RODNEY: Do you think I'll desert you?

BLAKE: In time.

RODNEY: Let me be the judge of that.

BLAKE: Do you love me?

RODNEY: Yes.

BLAKE: Why don't I believe you?

RODNEY: I thought you did.

BLAKE: Just because you gave me an expensive ring?

RODNEY: I don't believe in ceremonies.

BLAKE: Why do you make me wear tattered sweaters around the house? And this peculiar perfume? I don't understand your taste.

RODNEY: My taste is peculiar.

BLAKE: Why doesn't Catherine object?

RODNEY: Is she bothering you?

BLAKE: Not any more.

RODNEY: Good.

BLAKE: It doesn't sit well with me.

RODNEY: Must we worry about etiquette?

BLAKE: But Rodney...

RODNEY: Is it wrong to love a beautiful young girl?

BLAKE: I feel dirty.

RODNEY: When?

BLAKE: When she's around.

RODNEY: Catherine?

BLAKE: How many wives do you have?

RODNEY: Quite a few.

BLAKE: I don't like your humor.

RODNEY: Because of her southern upbringing, Catherine doesn't let me enjoy my jokes. I don't expect that from you.

BLAKE: I'm often tired of your jokes.

RODNEY: Alright. I now know better.

BLAKE: Do I remind you of Roberta?

RODNEY: Not in the slightest.

BLAKE: But there is a remarkable resemblance.

RODNEY: Says who?

BLAKE: Many of your associates.

RODNEY: Let them eat cake.

BLAKE: They think I control you.

RODNEY: You can dance on my heart.

BLAKE: Would you like that?

RODNEY: I don't know.

BLAKE: One day I might try.

RODNEY: You wouldn't harm a hair on my head.

BLAKE: Catherine might.

RODNEY: She would never. She's condoned everything. Given her blessings, in fact. I'm very proud of Catherine.

BLAKE: Is that why you keep the bedroom door ajar?

RODNEY: This evening you seem to be on a fact-finding mission.

BLAKE: You're evasive, Rodney.

RODNEY: It's called...mystique. Hasn't Catherine oriented you?

BLAKE: I've heard the entire Rodney lecture.

RODNEY: Has she told you everything?

BLAKE: You snore, play with trains, stain your silk hankies, butter with your steak knife, have difficulty with your fly, use rubber bands when you fall limp, limp a lot, hide girlie magazines in a financial portfolio, take bromides when you visit your mother on her birthday. That was my briefing.

RODNEY: A sterling briefing.

BLAKE: She treats me like a long lost relative.

RODNEY: You can repay her the kindness.

BLAKE: I will.

RODNEY: Is Catherine out this evening?

BLAKE: Yes.

RODNEY: Good.

BLAKE: You're feeling romantic?

RODNEY: Yes.

BLAKE: I'm not.

RODNEY: What a shame. Perhaps I'll take my nightly stroll, or play with my toy trains.

BLAKE: Who are you fooling?

RODNEY: Did you think...

BLAKE: A rape.

RODNEY: Out of the question. I've no strength today. And I take hormones. Depo-privera.

BLAKE: *(Recoiling from him)* I'm not kidding.

RODNEY: *(Controlling his behavior)* Then I'll apologize.

BLAKE: All sorts of V I Ps court you.

RODNEY: Are you surprised?

BLAKE: Yes.

RODNEY: Because I'm short and stocky? And part of the great turgid prose each election year? It's the bastard's need for philanthropy. I'm very generous with my time which makes all the difference. *(Approaching her again)* I love the delicate shape of your neck. I love the corners of your dainty mouth. I love your rough and tumble.

BLAKE: I don't like bedrooms.

RODNEY: Nor do I.

BLAKE: There are too many crucifixes in this apartment.

RODNEY: My dear wife sits on the bleachers with God.

BLAKE: Don't patronize me.

RODNEY: Whatever you say.

BLAKE: You'll have to stop drinking. *(Pause)* And stop these awful wet kisses. *(Pause)* And when you break wind, do it in private.

RODNEY: Blake.

BLAKE: Stop calling me that.

RODNEY: What shall I call you?

BLAKE: It's the sound of your voice.

RODNEY: I can't change that.

BLAKE: Try.

RODNEY: *(Softer)* Blake.

BLAKE: Again.

RODNEY: *(Fainter)* Blake.

BLAKE: All wrong. I'm not undressing.

RODNEY: I'll dim the light.

BLAKE: No.

RODNEY: We can fondle in the dark.

BLAKE: You mustn't touch me.

RODNEY: Take off that cardigan.

BLAKE: I hate men like you.

RODNEY: So do I. *(Hands touching her firmly)*

BLAKE: I'll hit back.

RODNEY: *(Absurd shift)* More bourbon, darling?

BLAKE: I'm not afraid to run away.

RODNEY: You are.

BLAKE: Just because you've crippled one girl, you can't cripple me.

RODNEY: Where would you go?

BLAKE: Back to school.

RODNEY: Admit it. You're unaffected by men your own age. I could set up a rent-controlled apartment on the east side.

BLAKE: No, I want something better.

RODNEY: There is nothing better, believe me.

BLAKE: You're a liar.

RODNEY: I'm a liar. So what. No one's offering trinkets.

BLAKE: Then what do I want?

RODNEY: An independent life.

BLAKE: No, that's not what you really think.

RODNEY: It's beyond words. Aside from the masquerade...

BLAKE: I don't want a doll house, Rodney.

RODNEY: *(Solemnly)* Marriage?

BLAKE: Perhaps.

RODNEY: A gauntlet?

BLAKE: Yes.

RODNEY: I thought so.

Scene Two

(Some days later. RODNEY's study)

CATHERINE: Why are you showing me these pictures? *(Photos in hand)*

BLAKE: Aren't you concerned?

CATHERINE: No.

BLAKE: I wanted to report on Roberta.

CATHERINE: Why?

BLAKE: It seemed appropriate.

CATHERINE: My husband put you up to this. *(Hands photos back.)* I don't care for pornography. Even with her clothes on.

BLAKE: She hasn't heard from you in six weeks.

CATHERINE: The separation will do her a world of good.

BLAKE: She's lost weight.

CATHERINE: Has she?

BLAKE: Thinner than ink. She's missed her period also.

CATHERINE: That's typical of her.

BLAKE: The orchestra's looking for her. Sometimes she doesn't get out of bed. The phone's off the hook. Yesterday I found her with the oven door open. I don't know your daughter that well, but I think she's in serious trouble.

CATHERINE: Roberta has a perverse sense of drama. If it's more grave, we'll just put her on medication.

BLAKE: It may be too late for that.

CATHERINE: It's never too late...for medication. Why take so much interest in Roberta?

BLAKE: Call it kinship.

CATHERINE: You've nothing in common with her.

BLAKE: It's as though I displaced her.

CATHERINE: Did she tell you that?

BLAKE: In so many words.

CATHERINE: She's very manipulative. I must caution you.

BLAKE: You discarded her like a stray.

CATHERINE: With a girl like Roberta, does one call the A S P C A? *(Pause)* Isn't she keeping company with an older man?

BLAKE: No.

CATHERINE: Perhaps she ought to go back to the mink farm?

BLAKE: She wants you to make a vat of soup.

CATHERINE: Whatever for?

BLAKE: For her consumption. Mother's soup, a miracle cure.

CATHERINE: Darling, there are no miracle cures.

BLAKE: Catherine, she wants to see you.

CATHERINE: I'm here.

BLAKE: You might pay her a visit.

CATHERINE: Do you insist?

BLAKE: I do. She's near anorexic.

CATHERINE: We can't have that, can we? Even if it's in style. *(Removes a fur from hall closet)* Give her this. No feeding required. Tell her to wear it indoors so no one can see her condition. *(Drapes coat over chair)* I wanted to collect precious stones around the world. We're absolutely mad about collecting. Rodney has his Lionel trains. I have my porcelain and china. Roberta, her scampy little animals. Our dinner service was always a problem. Something breaking every night. Roberta feeding her flock with my best china. Rodney's miniature railroad on my serving silver. What does one do when the entire family's obsessions coalesce on the dining room table? *(Stroking BLAKE's cheek)* Your make-up is quite lovely today.

BLAKE: Please don't touch me.

CATHERINE: Very well.

BLAKE: What have you done with my diaphram?

CATHERINE: Was that yours in the bath? *(Pause)* I used it to make strawberry preserves. I'm sorry, darling. I'll buy you another.

BLAKE: You enjoy playing these games, Catherine?

CATHERINE: Sometimes.

BLAKE: Perhaps you're sicker than Roberta?

CATHERINE: I doubt that very much. (*Pause*) Maybe I've too much time on my hands. I once took part in Rodney's office. Managed a good deal of it.

BLAKE: He said that your father started his career.

CATHERINE: There are many versions of that story.

BLAKE: Please tell me.

CATHERINE: I've no sense of history.

BLAKE: Your amnesia is selective.

CATHERINE: And so is yours. Do you employ mnemonic devices?

BLAKE: Rodney's cue cards.

CATHERINE: When we share these little secrets, I feel we forge a close bond. Even closer than your bond with Rodney. We are spoils of his ravenous appetite. Are we not in love with the same glutton?

BLAKE: How ugly you make it seem.

CATHERINE: Do I? I see only ribbons and bows, as I stare at his listless sleeping body.

BLAKE: If I were his wife...

CATHERINE: Perish the thought. Why would you want marriage when you already have access? Marriage is a series of unsightly stretch marks. I think I prefer religion in comparison. You can sense how vital a little string of beads can be. It's far better to marry God and tolerate His bits of neurosis. Dear girl, I've found faith and prayer the greatest power on earth. One day you will partake. (*Pause*) Young lady, you are my own special friend, my dear contessa, my devout and loyal witness. Do as you wish as long as Rodney's happy, and peace graces our sweet home.

BLAKE: Thank you, Catherine.

CATHERINE: Who says its a man's world? If Rodney
knew otherwise...though he's a remarkable instructor.
And so clever at his business. It's not power, my dear,
but perogative. And so you've permission to phone
the party leaders, attend caucuses, fly Ambassador,
perhaps visit the White House. Wouldn't you rather be
singing psalms?

BLAKE: I'm not staying for any more of it.

CATHERINE: Won't you?

BLAKE: No, Roberta's coming home this week.

CATHERINE: Is she?

BLAKE: Yes. Rodney knows.

CATHERINE: Again, I'm the last to know. She and
Rodney must be telepathic.

BLAKE: You don't seem happy about it.

CATHERINE: I'm relentlessly hard on her. Yet it is her
singular image which I love. Can you understand that?
She can change faces at her whim, though never age.
The years have been stern on us. Roberta challenged
me with every weapon in her arsenal. Does she think
she won by returning? I'd rather have a conflict in
heaven than an unmitigating migraine in my living
room. No, Roberta has not won. *(Pause)* When she was
a toddler she always had a peculiar way of sitting.
That's a sorority joke. *(Pause)* How often I wanted to
befriend her. To be her sister. To dress her myself.
To throw all her hurt and pain away. To nuture her
forever. How I encouraged her to nuture the cello and
to make sacrifices to it. How I stayed with her during
her first menstruation. Dare she forget these things?
How often she sabotaged every blind date I arranged.
How often I wanted to pop her little rodents into the
micro-wave. How often did I visit the hospitals and
clinics? Her illnesses blackmailed us. We paid too

much, we never stop paying. And I pay more than
anyone else. That's what's strangest about us. You see,
she's closer to her mother than even herself. Down to
rhythms and breaths. One pulse between us. My young
lost Roberta.

Scene Three

(Some days later. RODNEY *and* BLAKE *are in his study with*
CATHERINE *sitting within earshot.)*

RODNEY: To accentuate would be a mistake. We could
meet at the Biltmore, have drinks, go over the texts
with Victor and the boys, and perhaps make a polite
change or two. He likes you very much and I don't
mind if you end up toasting to each other's health.
Victor won't go further. I'd like you to wear something
low cut, and comb your hair to one side. Show your
beauty mark. You can kick off your shoes under the
table. Let's give them a good show. There's much
riding on this.

BLAKE: I can't make it.

RODNEY: What?

BLAKE: I'm sorry, Rodney. It's all over.

*(*RODNEY *turns to see* CATHERINE, *who shrugs passively.)*

RODNEY: What's wrong now?

BLAKE: Roberta's coming home.

RODNEY: So?

BLAKE: She calls me your whore of a mistress.

RODNEY: Excuse her humor. We all do.

BLAKE: She made me cry all day.

RODNEY: Why didn't you tell me this earlier?

BLAKE: I tried to hold it back. Catherine knows.

RODNEY: This meeting can't be postponed. Roberta can wait. Tell her to wait.

BLAKE: How can I?

RODNEY: Either you tell her, or I will.

BLAKE: She's threatening suicide.

RODNEY: If she tries anything foolish, we've no resort but to hospitalize her.

BLAKE: She'll tell the doctors everything.

RODNEY: There's nothing to tell.

BLAKE: She believes otherwise.

RODNEY: Who would believe her?

BLAKE: Do you really want to risk it?

RODNEY: No one threatens me. Not even my own daughter.

CATHERINE: May I say something, darling?

RODNEY: Yes?

CATHERINE: I saw her this morning. She's in awful shape.

RODNEY: That bad?

CATHERINE: Cancel the Biltmore appointment.

RODNEY: Alright.

CATHERINE: Meet with Roberta.

RODNEY: I will. Where is she now?

CATHERINE: Downstairs.

RODNEY: Catherine, is it safe to leave her alone?

CATHERINE: No.

RODNEY: Keep her occupied.

CATHERINE: I'd rather not.

RODNEY: Does she want to stay?

CATHERINE: It's gotten beyond that. Why don't you ask her yourself?

RODNEY: Quite frankly, she frightens me at these times. Should we call the hospital?

CATHERINE: I really don't know any more.

BLAKE: Shall I see her up?

RODNEY: Thank you. In the meantime, we should make some phone calls. *(To* BLAKE*)* Throw something on. You should look a little neater.

*(*BLAKE *exits.)*

CATHERINE: I'm not happy about this.

RODNEY: We have to make some adjustments, Catherine.

CATHERINE: Do you want her to move back?

RODNEY: If the child's in pain, what can we do? You talked with her.

CATHERINE: She's greatly disturbed.

RODNEY: I see no other alternative.

CATHERINE: Then Blake must go.

RODNEY: Then she goes.

CATHERINE: But if Roberta is to stay, she must stop play acting.

RODNEY: How do you propose to stop her habit?

CATHERINE: We must find her a husband.

RODNEY: You seem indifferent.

CATHERINE: No, I still care.

RODNEY: Splendid.

CATHERINE: To hell with your sarcasm, Rodney.

RODNEY: Thank God you have our interest at heart.

CATHERINE: One of us must be the sober parent.

RODNEY: And the Lord assigned that role to you.

CATHERINE: *(Flatly)* He did.

RODNEY: It is a dubious distinction, Catherine.

CATHERINE: You're not going to have your way every time. You better pray she keeps a discreet silence.

RODNEY: I am praying.

CATHERINE: And ask for clemency, Rodney. Genuflect.

RODNEY: Must I?

CATHERINE: You must. Some devil's got you by the heart.

(ROBERTA enters wearing CATHERINE's fur. She appears gaunt.)

ROBERTA: *(In a daze)* Hello, Daddy.

RODNEY: *(With effort)* Hello, Roberta. What did you do to your hair?

ROBERTA: Henna. It'll grow out.

RODNEY: Come closer, sweetheart. Let me look at you.

ROBERTA: *(Frozen movement)* I have lice. Or ear mites. Rabid thoughts. Can you hear them? *(Pause)* Are you mad at me?

RODNEY: No, darling. Why would I be? *(He stands, approaches her.)* Give me your coat.

ROBERTA: Do you want to dance?

RODNEY: No.

ROBERTA: Do you want me to sit on your knee?

RODNEY: No.

ROBERTA: You don't know what banishment feels like, Daddy.

RODNEY: I think I do.

ROBERTA: It's a Munch painting hung upside down in Hell, where the walls blister and the fumes puss. It's a dish of De-Con poison in your school lunch. It's a black birthday card from Catherine The Great, with wishes none too pleasant. She weened me on chloroform, though my recollection is excellent.

RODNEY: Darling, shouldn't we see a doctor?

ROBERTA: Heavens, no! They'll tap my head with their little rubber hammers. Write me a column, Daddy. Make me a star. We'll dine in Paris fashion, and fashion all night long. *(She dances a minuet.)* If you prefer the other girl, I'll be very bitter. Such surface beauty can't be everything. Good breeding offers more. We look for traces of Nature in Her truest face. We look for that seed which is not a spore. We want no weeds in our garden. *(Approaching* RODNEY*)* I don't grant favors any more. I won't bruise my knees for you. I shall not be scraped clean for my baby shower. I can never conceive. I'll not hide my moodiness nor my bowlegged walk. I shall not reproach myself.

CATHERINE: Maybe you'll grace us with a recital, Roberta?

ROBERTA: A recital, Catherine?

CATHERINE: I would love to hear you play.

ROBERTA: Look at my hands. They've grown extra knuckles. They move by themselves.

CATHERINE: Stop imagining things, darling. Your hands are fine.

*(*ROBERTA*'s fingers are now pulsated.)*

CATHERINE: Only a child pretends these sort of things. You're not a child now. Don't worry us so.

ROBERTA: Wake me.

RODNEY: How can we?

ROBERTA: You know how.

RODNEY: No, tell me.

ROBERTA: Under the quilt, under the pillow, under my pajamas, under me. Rock me. Rock me. Catherine's out of the house. Another stuffed toy on my bed. Who is this creature, Daddy?

RODNEY: Don't rekindle bad dreams, Roberta.

ROBERTA: Who is this creature? Why is he touching me?

RODNEY: *(Seeing her physical discomfort, he puts his arm around her.)* You're quivering.

ROBERTA: I put all my feelings in a bottle. The safest place to put them. I'm only trying to be practical. In my wardrobe there are too many people. In my mirror there is a stranger. In the hallway Catherine rearranges the line of antiques. Why did she do this to me?

CATHERINE: Nothing has changed in this home, Roberta. It's exactly as it was.

ROBERTA: Even the windows are inverted. Nothing looks out. Where are the neighbors.

CATHERINE: Your hysterics are manufactured.

ROBERTA: My hysterics are your heirlooms. You can have them back.

CATHERINE: It's wrong, Roberta. I need your love. Isn't that a reflection of something? Don't rant on like some mad orphan.

ROBERTA: You're an accomplice to a greater madness, Catherine.

CATHERINE: I'm still an attractive woman.

ROBERTA: As warm as a marble bust. I am in awe of you.

RODNEY: Show me a sign of renewal.

ROBERTA: On my terms.

RODNEY: On your terms.

ROBERTA: You know my terms clearly.

RODNEY: Those terms are impossible.

ROBERTA: Try harder, Daddy.

RODNEY: Do you want us all to be crazy?

ROBERTA: Yes.

RODNEY: We are intimate, Roberta. Can't you accept that?

ROBERTA: She kicks and I rear. Enough, please. Take ten pints of blood. My head's about to burst. What a ghastly sonata, Catherine.

CATHERINE: Why don't you put on your slippers and bring down your cello?

ROBERTA: I can't play any more, damn you all.

RODNEY: You've never left home, darling. This was always your home.

ROBERTA: Why should I believe you now?

RODNEY: Because I am repentant.

ROBERTA: Show me.

RODNEY: Over time.

ROBERTA: Now.

RODNEY: You have my word, Roberta.

(ROBERTA *exits slowly.*)

CATHERINE: You cannot keep fooling the child.

RODNEY: I don't intend to. We'll go back to a more perfect period. (*Pause*) Have I acted wisely?

CATHERINE: Isn't that rather late to ask?

RODNEY: When should I have asked?

CATHERINE: Twenty years ago.

RODNEY: You exaggerate, Catherine.

CATHERINE: You don't see any gravity to it, Rodney.
I go to confession in total shambles. Where do you
confess?

RODNEY: Confess to what? *(Pause)* I'm not a Catholic,
thank God.

CATHERINE: Still very satisfied, how do you keep aloof?

RODNEY: The two of you frighten me. You know I'm
frightened.

CATHERINE: I see postures and nothing else. *(Pause)*
Rodney, you're an actor.

RODNEY: Only to entertain you.

CATHERINE: It will catch up to you.

RODNEY: I've gotten my telegram from Hell. Have you
received yours?

CATHERINE: Yes.

RODNEY: We're due for a respite from our little ghosts.
We could have played this differently. Why didn't
you?

CATHERINE: I didn't care what you did out of town
with her.

RODNEY: Your apology is in order.

CATHERINE: How can I apologize?

RODNEY: Let go of your rosary and mouth the words,
darling.

CATHERINE: No, I cannot. *(Pause. Walking aimlessly.)*
Our secrets have died and our plans have become
slightly monstrous. Roberta has returned no older
than yesterday. Her scars show only your handiwork.

Nothing in the animal kingdom demands this much love and parenting.

RODNEY: Some children stay children forever.

CATHERINE: Are you one of them?

RODNEY: Forgive me. I won't be lenient with her. But Catherine, how are we going to change this child? She does what she pleases. She can't be trained. We knew this. Won't you please give me a sign, darling?

CATHERINE: There are no more signs.

RODNEY: I see many signs. Roberta will return to her music, relive her childhood, retreat. We can watch over her, give her shelter from the things she fears. Such is the order of things. (*Silence*) When you and I courted we had great expectations. Perhaps it's time for us to change. Twisted shadows pass.

(RODNEY *kisses* CATHERINE. *After a moment, they seat themselves in the living room—having set up a music stand and chair.* ROBERTA *enters wearing* CATHERINE's *wedding Gown. She carries her cello and walks with some apprehension to the chair. She fidgets with her dress and adjusts her veil. She stares ahead vacantly, waits for coaxing. Silence. Finally she prepares to play. The bow lifts and we hear Mendelssohn. After a few bars she falters and freezes. Blood is seen spilling mysteriously from below the cello. Silence. Lights fade to blackout.*)

END OF PLAY

www.ingramcontent.com/pod-product-compliance
Lightning Source LLC
Chambersburg PA
CBHW070032110426
42741CB00035B/2746